A
gift
honoring
Griffin
and
Carson
Gilchrist

COMICS AND GRAPHIC NOVELS

Richard Spilsbury

Heinemann Library
Chicago, Illinois

© 2007 Heinemann Library
a division of Reed Elsevier Inc.
Chicago, Illinois

Customer Service 888-454-2279
Visit our website at www.heinemannraintree.com

Produced for Heinemann Library by
White-Thomson Publishing Ltd.
Designed by Tim Mayer
Printed and bound in China by South China Printing Company.

11 10 09 08 07
10 9 8 7 6 5 4 3 2 1

Library of Congress Cataloging-in-Publication Data
Spilsbury, Richard, 1963-
  Comics and graphic novels / Richard Spilsbury.
    p. cm. -- (Art off the wall)
  Includes index.
  ISBN-10: 1-4034-8286-1 (library binding-hardcover)
  1. Comic books, strips, etc.--Authorship--Juvenile literature. 2. Graphic
novels--Authorship--Juvenile literature. I. Title. II. Series.
  PN6710.S65 2006
  741.5'1--dc22
                        2006005741

Acknowledgments
The publishers would like to thank the following for their kind permission to use their photographs:
akg-images pp. **5** (Universal TV/20th Century Fox), **51** (Pixar/Walt Disney/Album); Bridgeman Art Library p. **27**; Corbis pp. **12** (Amet Jean Pierre), **13** (Arne Dedert/epa), **16** (Ted Streshinsky), **23** (Fonlupt Gilles), **26**, **40** (Bojan Brecelj); Steve Galgas p. **41**; Getty Images pp. **17** (AFP), **46–47**, **48**; Last Resort Picture Library pp. **24–25**; Photolibrary p. **19**; TopFoto pp. **10** (ImageWorks), **49**; James Turner pp. **39**, **45**; Vinmag Archive Ltd pp. **4**, **6**, **7**, **9**, **11**, **15**, **20**, **21**, **29**, **30**, **32–33**, **35**, **36**, **43**; Ben Williams p. **31**.

The artwork on pages 37 and 42 was created by Peter Bull Art Studio.

Cover photograph reproduced with permission of Photolibrary.

Every effort has been made to contact copyright holders of any material reproduced in this book. Any omissions will be rectified in subsequent printings if notice is given to the publishers.

Contents

Words appearing in the text in bold, **like this**, are explained in the Glossary.

What Are Comics and Graphic Novels?

Most people have an idea what a comic is—for example, the short row of drawings called a **comic strip** at the bottom of a newspaper page, or a magazine or **comic book** filled with the colorful adventures of different characters. Whatever the type, comics are all made up of pictures arranged in a definite order. Comics are sometimes defined as "**sequential art**."

The separate pictures in a comic always have things in common, such as the same characters or settings. However, a few things change from one picture to the next, such as the position of a character. The arrangement, or **layout**, of the pictures is planned to make readers follow what is changing between one picture and the next. The pictures usually also have words within or right next to them to help explain the action.

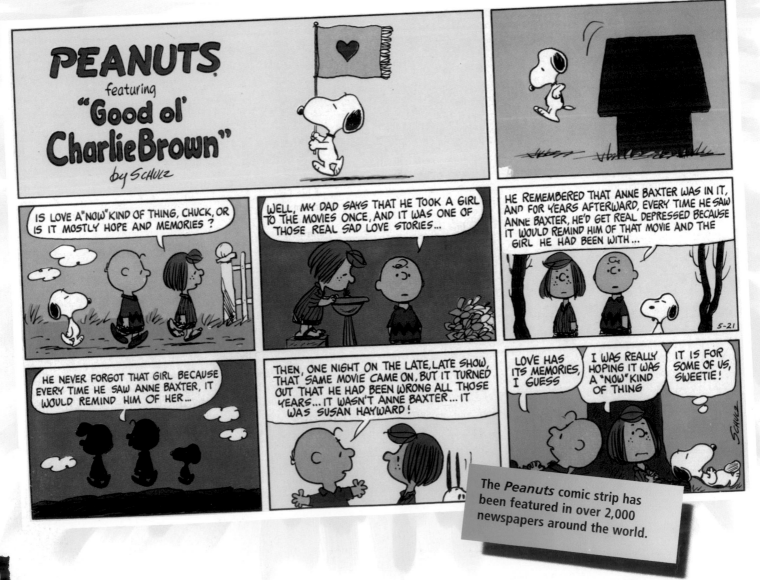

The *Peanuts* comic strip has been featured in over 2,000 newspapers around the world.

Graphic novels

Graphic novels are simply comics planned as longer books. They often have a more in-depth story that moves among different settings. Usually graphic novels feature a much wider range of characters than shorter comics. Some of the pictures may be very detailed and may take up whole pages. Some graphic novels are actually collections of stories created and originally published at different times, but always featuring the adventures of the same characters.

Tricks of the trade

You can easily get caught up in a good comic just as you can in a good book. Some of the characters and the fascinating places in their world might appeal to you. Maybe the story is so gripping you cannot bear to put the comic down.

Throughout this book there will be lots of examples of the techniques different comic artists and writers use to convert their ideas into finished comics. When they have been successful, you should care what happens to their characters and believe in the drawn worlds they have invented.

Comic book characters often have features that make them stand out from the crowd. The easily recognizable Simpsons family is featured in a monthly comic book series based on the popular animated TV show *The Simpsons*.

Try it yourself

This book provides lots of activities you can try yourself. Most are simple exercises that relate to particular stages in the creation of comics—for example, how to draw eye shapes for different moods and how to change a story into pictures.

The aim is for you to build up enough skills to start making your own comics. You can use the completed exercises as part of a comic **portfolio**. This is a collection that you keep of your best and most recent work. It is a record of your development as a comic creator.

Picture This!

You stumble down to breakfast and spot a comic on the cereal box. Waiting for the school bus, you spot another one on an advertising poster. At school you open your Spanish workbook, and there is another comic. Sequences of pictures are all around us today. However, they are not a new way of telling stories and spreading information.

Early picture stories

The first picture stories we know of date back tens of thousands of years. Cave paintings show hunters, the wild animals they hunted, and dramatic moments when they fought their prey. These paintings were probably intended to record events and teach other people about hunting.

Other early picture stories are records of war and conquest. The famous Bayeux Tapestry, commissioned by a French bishop, tells the story of the Battle of Hastings, England, in 1066. The French army led by William killed the English king, Harold, and defeated his forces. France ruled England for the next 88 years.

The Bayeux Tapestry is a 230-foot- (70-meter-) long picture story embroidered nearly 1,000 years ago in thread on woolen cloth.

The *Eagle* comic book was very popular in the United Kingdom in the 1950s and 1960s. Dan Dare was a fearless pilot of the future who had adventures on strange planets.

Glass comics!

Inside most cathedrals or churches, colored light floods into the dark interior through stained-glass windows. Many of these windows are divided up into separate pictures, telling different stories about Jesus or the lives of saints. Many early churchgoers could not read. They learned about Biblical stories by looking at stained-glass windows.

The funnies

Strips of drawings first appeared in print in the early 19th century. They were often called "funnies" because they featured funny-looking people in humorous situations. Some characters were made-up, but others were recognizable **caricatures** of politicians and important people. By around 1900 they became known as "comics" rather than funnies.

Comic strips in print

In the early 20th century, comic strips featuring different adventures of the same characters were featured in many newspapers. By the 1930s some comic characters, such as Popeye, Dick Tracy, Flash Gordon, Blondie, and Li'l Abner, were becoming popular. Readers wanted to see more of their favorite characters' adventures, so different comic strips were often published together in comic books.

Unlucky in love

The first printed graphic novel appeared in 1837 in Europe. It was called *The Adventures of Obadiah Oldbuck* and it was created by Rodolphe Töpffer, a Swiss artist. In it, Oldbuck makes a complete fool of himself in his attempts to charm a woman who is not interested in him!

7

Birth of superheroes

Life in the United States during the 1930s was hard. There was mass unemployment and lots of poverty. This was the time when comics featuring **superhero** characters started to become very popular. Superheroes have special abilities to do improbable things. They were just the right characters to help people at that time to escape from reality.

The first popular superhero, Superman, was created by Jerry Siegel and Joe Shuster in 1938. Superman had astonishing strength and speed, the power to fly, amazing vision, and other unusual abilities. He wore a tight blue costume with a large "S" for "Superman" on the front. Superman fought crime whenever he was needed, but spent the rest of his life as Clark Kent, a clumsy, quiet reporter. The success of Superman encouraged lots of comic publishers to create their own superheroes, such as Batman, the Atom, and Wonderwoman.

More superheroes

In the late 1940s, when readers were ready for a bit more realism, a new kind of superhero became popular. One of these was "the Spirit," created by Will Eisner. The Spirit, a crime-fighter, was the half-living spirit of a detective. He dressed as an ordinary man wearing a mask. Rather than having super powers, the Spirit had ordinary human failings and fears.

Superheroes fell out of favor for a time, but in the 1960s Marvel Comics (see page 22) and DC Comics revived public interest in them. Marvel gained success with *Spiderman, The Fantastic Four, The Incredible Hulk, Captain America, X-Men*, and more, while DC found success with *Superman, Batman, Wonder Woman, The Green Lantern*, and others. Many of these series continue today.

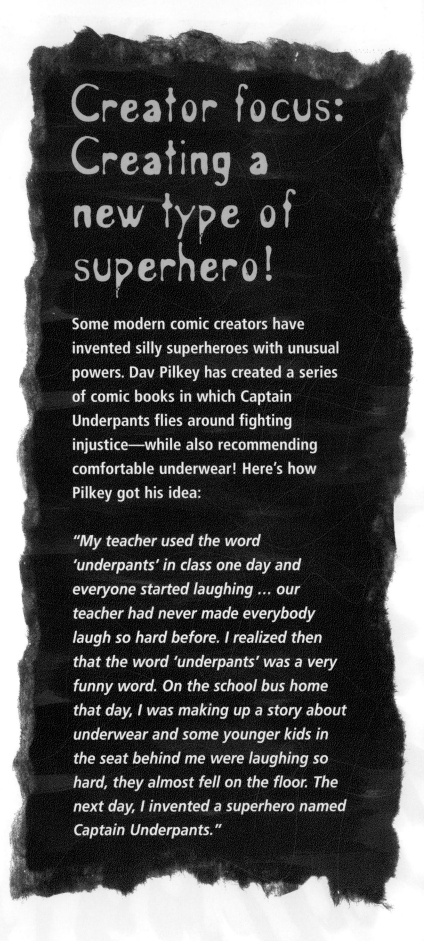

Creator focus: Creating a new type of superhero!

Some modern comic creators have invented silly superheroes with unusual powers. Dav Pilkey has created a series of comic books in which Captain Underpants flies around fighting injustice—while also recommending comfortable underwear! Here's how Pilkey got his idea:

"My teacher used the word 'underpants' in class one day and everyone started laughing ... our teacher had never made everybody laugh so hard before. I realized then that the word 'underpants' was a very funny word. On the school bus home that day, I was making up a story about underwear and some younger kids in the seat behind me were laughing so hard, they almost fell on the floor. The next day, I invented a superhero named Captain Underpants."

CAPTAIN UNDERPANTS
AND THE BIG, BAD BATTLE OF THE BIONIC BOOGER BOY
PART 1: THE NIGHT OF THE NASTY NOSTRIL NUGGETS

SQUISHY ACTION!

SMOOSHY HORROR!

GOOEY LAFFS!

THE SIXTH EPIC NOVEL
BY DAV PILKEY

Captain Underpants's costume is a cape and an enormous pair of white underpants!

SCHOLASTIC

9

Virtues of visuals

As young children, many of us learn to read using picture books. The pictures help us understand what words look like and what they mean. For example, a picture of a cat next to the word "cat" reinforces the definition of the word.

Sequences of images continue to be useful throughout our lives for showing us things and helping us remember them. For example, if you have been on an airplane, you will probably have seen instructions about how to put on a lifejacket in an emergency. The added advantage of not using words is that there is no need to translate the safety instructions into lots of languages for different passengers from around the world.

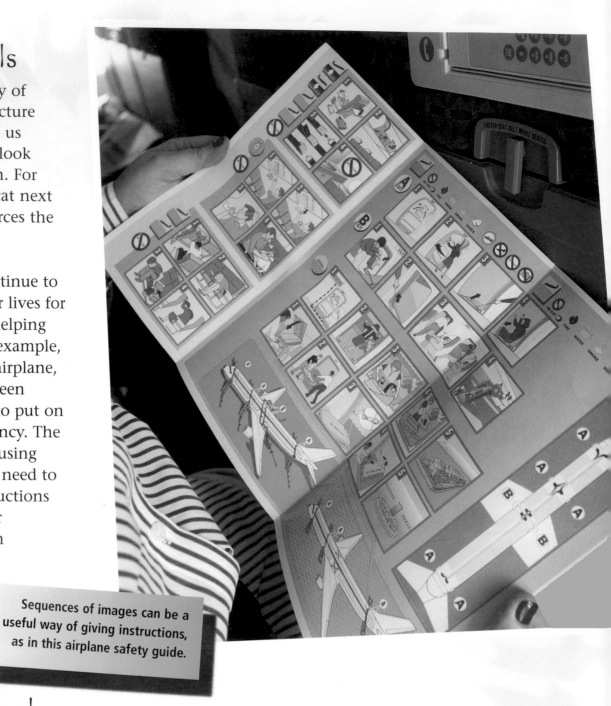

Sequences of images can be a useful way of giving instructions, as in this airplane safety guide.

Comics and school

Many adults read comics and graphic novels, but there is no doubt that they appeal most of all to younger people. That is why they can be a really useful educational tool. The impact of pictures used with just a few words makes complicated information more memorable and easier to understand. For example, plays by William Shakespeare can be difficult to read, since they are long and full of complicated language. Comic versions of the plays are much shorter.

They reduce the plots to their simplest forms and make relationships between characters clearer. Some people think that studying a comic version makes reading the original easier.

Comics can help us understand nonfiction such as science, too. For example, *Sandwalk Adventures* by Jay Hosler is a comic book about the complex theory of evolution, starring Charles Darwin and a talking parasite!

Serious messages

Some people think of comics and graphic novels largely as entertainment because they are often full of talking animals and dramatic battles. However, many also contain a serious message. For example, *The Lorax* by Dr. Seuss is all about habitat destruction and *V for Vendetta* by Alan Moore is about the dangers of too much government control.

Superman teaches vocabulary!

The use of comics in education began in the 1940s, when comic magazines were read by 95 percent of all 8- to 14-year-olds. When educators developed a Superman language workbook in 1944, which used comic strips to teach new words, teachers reported "unusual interest" in literacy among their students!

Shakespeare's *Hamlet* is easier to read as a comic than as lines of script.

ALAS, POOR YORICK! I KNEW HIM; A FELLOW OF INFINITE JEST, OF MOST EXCELLENT FANCY. HE HATH BORNE ME ON HIS BACK A THOUSAND TIMES. WHERE BE YOUR JIBES NOW, YOUR GAMBOLS, YOUR FLASHES OF MERRIMENT?

Manga are very widely read in Japan and other parts of the world.

Graphic novels

For some people, the term "graphic" or "visual novel" should only be used for certain long comic books. These contain images whose quality and style demonstrate excellent artistic ability. They should also be written for adults, with complicated stories spread over dozens of pages. Some people believe graphic novels are the visual equivalent of literature, which can reveal different things each time you read them, whereas most comic books are only read once. At the beginning of the 21st century, comic book sales are falling, while sales of graphic novels are rising.

World of comics

There are comics and graphic novels published in different countries all around the world. You will probably be familiar with many U.S. comics. For example, you have probably seen comics featuring Batman and the Simpsons. But how about comics from other places?

In Europe, popular comic books and graphic novels include the Belgian character Tintin and the French character Asterix.

Comics from Japan are called **manga**. There are different styles of manga suitable for different audiences. For example, the style of manga for young teenage boys is called **Shonen**. Other styles of Asian comics are created in China, Korea, and India. Indian comics range from depictions of religious stories to *Spiderman India*, in which the hero takes on demons from Hindu myths!

Translations and syndication

Comics have so few words that they are fairly easily translated into other languages. For example, *Asterix* books have been translated into 110 languages. Many U.S. comics have been **syndicated** around the world.

This means other newspapers and magazines pay for the right to use them. The most syndicated comic strip is *Garfield*, created by Jim Davis in 1978. It has appeared in 2,570 different publications worldwide.

French comic book creator Albert Uderzo stands next to a board featuring Asterix and Obelix, after publishing *Gaul in Danger* worldwide in 2005. This was the 33rd volume in the series.

Try it yourself

Garfield is a comic strip about a grumpy cat. Why don't you make your own version? Draw a row of three or four boxes and think up an idea for your cat. For example, the cat is outside and sees its food inside. It runs at the cat door, but it is locked. Draw simple pictures with a black pen to show your story without using any words.

Parts of a comic

Different types of comic can look very different, but they usually contain the same elements:

- **Panels:** These are the square or rectangular boxes where the action takes place. Panels are similar to the view through a camera, through a window, or onto a movie screen. What you see is a **background** against which characters talk and create the action. Most panels in comics are arranged in lines across the page, so we can read them as we would lines of words in a book. However, some comic creators devise unusual page layouts with, for example, panels within panels to tell their stories.

- **Gutters:** The narrow spaces or lines between the panels are called gutters. Gutters separate panels and can indicate a shift in time and place.

- **Word bubbles:** These are the rounded or rectangular white spaces that display what the characters say to each other (the **dialogue**), what they think, and sometimes what they are feeling.

- **Captions:** These are the boxes above or below panels that contain text. They are often headings or titles, but sometimes they explain what has happened before the action begins. This is called the **backstory**.

Closure

In one panel, a strong-looking baseball pitcher pulls back her pitching arm holding the ball. In the next panel, the batter looks in shock at his splintered bat. You automatically fill in the missing piece of action—the pitch was so fast it broke the bat. Even though the comic does not show this piece of the action, you know what happened. The way we fill in the gaps between one image and the next is called closure.

The gutters between panels have a very important job in any comic. They are the parts that make the reader produce closure. Depending on what is drawn in the panels, a gutter can mean a shift in time or place. The baseball example given above shows a shift in time. Comic creators can use gutters to help them cut down on how much action they actually have to draw.

Try it yourself

When we read a comic strip, our imaginations fill in the gaps in the action between the panels, producing closure. But how much closure can comic creators expect of their readers? Try this exercise with your friends.

Find a comic strip in an old newspaper or photocopy one from a comic book. Cut the strip into separate panels. Remove some of the panels from the middle of the strip and tape the remaining panels together again. Show the new strip to your friends. Can they make sense of the shortened story?

Some comic books, such as Raymond Briggs's *The Snowman*, have almost no words. The action is shown just through the pictures. The gutters between the panels show shifts in time and place, and the reader's imagination fills in the gaps in the action.

Tools of the trade

Before you begin drawing, you will need the right tools to do it neatly. In the past, comic and graphic novel artists always used traditional art equipment. They drew panels on good quality cardboard called Bristol board, which had no loose fibers that could make the ink lines smudge. They used pens or fine brushes dipped in black India ink to draw accurate lines. Any mistakes were covered using white ink. They carefully added colored paint where necessary. Many artists used plastic or metal **templates** to add lettering to word bubbles and rulers to draw straight lines. Some people still draw comics this way today.

The comic artist Charles Schultz, creator of the *Peanuts* comic strip, inks over the penciled-in characters. *Peanuts*, featuring the characters Charlie Brown and his dog, Snoopy, first appeared in 1950 and became one of the most popular comic strips of all time.

Comic art on the computer

Today, many comic and graphic novel artists use **computer graphics software** such as *PaintShop Pro* or *Illustrator* to produce finished drawings. They use computers with similar amounts of memory to the ones you might find at school or in your home, but with large, **high-resolution** screens so that they can see their pictures well. Some comic artists draw outlines of characters with a pen on paper and then scan them into a computer to make digital versions of their drawings. Others draw outlines on-screen using a plastic pen on a **graphics tablet** connected to a computer.

It is easy to **manipulate** digital outlines once you have opened them within the graphics software. For example, you can enlarge, reduce, stretch, rotate, or erase lines and shapes with a few clicks of the mouse.

You can add, change, and remove colors and patterns very easily. Many people create finished drawings of characters and then export them into special page layout software such as *QuarkXpress*. This makes it easy to create different panel shapes and adjust the look of the page until it is just right.

Traditional or digital?

Some people prefer the handcrafted look of traditionally produced comics. They say the imperfections and variation in ink lines and coloring reveal the artist's style, whereas computer lines and color look too uniform and a bit bland. Other people say the creative possibilities on computers are endless. However, whichever **medium** you choose, the important things are to have a good story, good characters, and an appealing layout.

Many comic creators scan their illustrations into computers and then use graphics software to produce the finished versions. Here, artist Jeevan J. Kang works on a digital image of Spiderman for an Indian version of the classic comic.

First Steps Toward a Comic

Picture a comic strip. Panel one shows a budding comic artist sitting and staring at a blank piece of paper, with pencil poised. Panel two shows a clock. Panel three shows the same clock 10 minutes later. Panel four shows that the paper is still blank. Coming up with a good story and characters is the first step toward creating a comic or graphic novel.

Comic plots

Some experts say there are only a limited number of basic plots in the world, and that most stories are variations on these themes. For example, "rags to riches" is the basic plot in the story of Cinderella, and "overcoming the monster" is the plot in the movie *Jaws*, where the monster is a great white shark. Comic writers, like any other writers, use some of these basic plots in stories they make up. However, they often adapt existing stories.

Typical well-known sources of stories for comic plots are myths and fairy tales, classic literature such as the stories of Mark Twain or the plays of William Shakespeare, and historical events. Whatever your source or inspiration, the important thing is to tell the story in your own way.

Recycling comic stories

Sometimes comic creators recycle stories used in previous comics. For example, *Dark Knight Returns* by Frank Miller, written in 1985, is a grittier and darker version of the original *Batman* comic of the late 1930s. It features the same characters as the original, but focuses on different aspects of the story, such as why Batman should have become a committed crime-fighter in the first place. Each category of manga recycles certain kinds of plot and features certain types of character.

A manga story

Shonen manga for young teenage boys often feature outsiders in fairly normal settings. *Wonder 3* by the comic artist Osamu Tezuka is a fairly typical Shonen manga story. Shinichi, the main character, is a troubled teenager. He fights, skips school, and has no friends. That is, until aliens sent to observe Earth become his best friends. We can soon see through his aggressive character and realize he feels very vulnerable. He does not get into fights because he is bad, but rather because he cannot stand to see the unfairness of the adult world. That is his way of battling against corruption and greed. In the end, Shinichi saves the world through his bravery and loyalty. Phew!

Manga comics feature many different types of story aimed at different readers. Manga that are aimed at teenage boys often feature action adventure stories.

All about me

Many creators of comics include a bit about themselves in their drawings and words. Some comics depict the events that have taken place in the author's life. An example of this type of **autobiographical** comic is *Persepolis* by Marjane Satrapi. It shows the creator as a small girl growing up in Iran at a time when the society was very strict about what girls were allowed to wear and do. Other autobiographical artists include R. Crumb and Harvey Pekar.

Some autobiographical comics try to show how the author feels about something. For example, *Epileptic* by David B. is about a young boy whose elder brother has **epilepsy**. The young boy sees epilepsy as a monster taking over his brother at first, but as he grows up the monster becomes part of his brother. Drawings can often express an author's feelings in a way that words alone cannot.

Let's talk about issues

It is sometimes easier to talk about serious things indirectly. **Allegory** is when authors and artists use fictional characters and events to symbolize real ones. Comic creators sometimes use allegory to deal with issues such as Nazism, racism, and terrorism.

In *The Hooded Hordes* (1938) by Jerry Siegel and Joe Shuster, the main characters investigate and expose a white-hooded terrorist organization. The Hooded Hordes are a fictional version of a real-life racist group called the Ku Klux Klan. Some types of allegory disguise real people as different creatures, as in Art Spiegelman's graphic novel *Maus*.

In this panel, Marjane Satrapi shows how she felt divided as a child between her traditional culture and new influences.

I REALLY DIDN'T KNOW WHAT TO THINK ABOUT THE VEIL. DEEP DOWN I WAS VERY RELIGIOUS BUT AS A FAMILY WE WERE VERY MODERN AND AVANT-GARDE.

Creator focus: Art Spiegelman's Maus

Art Spiegelman was born in 1948 and has been a comic artist since he was a teenager. His parents survived the Nazi concentration camp at Auschwitz, but his mother was so troubled by the memories that she killed herself. In 1986 Spiegelman created a graphic novel called *Maus* that was all about his parents' experiences. It is a very sad tale about suffering, and also about the difficulty of relating to other people after the war.

Spiegelman uses different types of animal as allegories of the different races and nationalities of the characters. For example, Jewish characters are drawn as mice and Germans are cats. He chose animals partly because Nazis talked about other races as if they were animals rather than people. *Maus* was the first graphic novel to win a **Pulitzer Prize** for literature.

In *Maus* Adolf Hitler is depicted as a cat and his Jewish victims as mice.

From story to script

Once you have your story, you need to think about how you can show it in comic form. You will need to decide what length the comic will be. Then, you need to divide up the story idea into the number of panels you will have.

Many comic creators produce a detailed **script** for their comic, although some make a less-detailed **synopsis**. A script or synopsis is a written description of which part of the story happens in each panel.

Scenes

Just like the scripts of plays or movies, comic scripts are broken up into **scenes**. A typical opening scene shows normal life for the main characters. The following scenes build up suspense before reaching a big action climax, such as a fight scene. The last scenes return things to normal or hint at future adventures.

Layout tips

A rough layout is a sketch of the story in pictures and words that follows the script or synopsis. This is probably the most important planning stage in creating a comic, so here are some helpful tips:

- You are going to make mistakes, so use a pencil and have an eraser ready

- Your pictures at this stage can be little more than stick people or rough blobs

- Use a large opening panel with a detailed drawing to set the scene

- When there is a lot of action, use many panels on the same page so the page looks busier

- Leave space for word bubbles and captions

- In a multipage comic, try to end each page with the end of a scene. Also try to use cliffhangers, which are exciting points in the story that hint at further action.

Creator focus: The Marvel method

Stan Lee is one of the most famous comic writers. He made Marvel Comics into a major worldwide comic publisher. He could not have put together comics without artist collaborators such as Jack Kirby. Together, Lee and Kirby created *The Fantastic Four*, *X-Men*, and *The Incredible Hulk*.

Kirby and Lee started by **brainstorming** a basic story together before Lee came up with a brief synopsis. Then, Kirby laid out the story panel by panel in pencil across the number of pages they needed to fill. Lee added word bubbles before Kirby used ink to draw in final pictures that Lee colored in. This way of working in a team is often called the Marvel method.

This comic artist is laying out the panels in which he will present the action.

Try it yourself

It is time to try laying out an action comic. You could make this about an unusual or special thing that has happened to you. Set yourself a limit of 16 panels containing four scenes.

You will need:

● Notepaper for planning

● Large pieces of drawing paper

● A sharp pencil, an eraser, and a sharpener

● A ruler.

1 The story

First, you need to think of an idea for the story. Perhaps you fell off a chair and broke your arm, or maybe you got a phone call saying you had won tickets to see your favorite band. Whatever your story is, it will need to have a plot, settings, characters, and dialogue. Other characters might include pets, family members, teachers, friends, or even mysterious strangers. Remember, the story should be told from your point of view. Write your idea on some notepaper.

2 The script

Now, produce a script or synopsis for your comic by dividing the story into four scenes. The first scene shows what the normal situation is. The second scene shows the reason why the situation changed. For example, you lean back on a chair, or the phone rings. Scene three is where the unusual thing happens. Make this part full of action and exciting. It is, after all, the point of the story. The last scene shows what happened after the event, as life returned to normal, or as life was changed forever. Plan what was said in each scene. You may clearly remember the actual dialogue, but if not, just make it up as the characters may have said it.

Before you put pencil to paper and draw any layout, you should plan what is going to happen, to whom, and what is said in each panel.

3 The layout

Next, plan the layout. Use the ruler to draw a grid of 16 equal sized, rectangular panels. Have four rows of four rectangles. It is up to you whether you have gutters between them. Now, start to draw in the panels following your script. Remember to sketch in figures roughly. Do you need to leave space for word bubbles? Will the action become clearer with some backstory in a separate caption?

Going further

You can create a finished comic quickly using special software such as *Comic Book Creator* (see page 55). This software has lots of built-in characters you can use, templates for many different panel arrangements, and lots of backgrounds and text styles to make your comic look exciting. You can also import pictures you have drawn or pictures you find on the Internet.

Developing Comic Characters

It is important to decide on a layout, but what will the characters look like in the final comic? After all, these are the main elements in each panel. Developing the look of characters can take some time. But if you get it right, your readers will be drawn into the action.

Cartoon features

Take a look at a few different comic characters and you will probably agree that most do not look particularly realistic. This is not because the artists cannot draw well. It is done on purpose to give the characters more impact. Many comics are drawn as cartoons. These are stylized drawings where bodily proportions are changed for effect.

Features are often simplified. For example, cartoon faces may have enlarged eyes and the mouth, nose, and ears may be reduced to very simple curves. They may have none of the facial lines and creases we have in reality. Simplification helps the reader identify the emotions of characters. The main parts of the face that show emotions are the eyes and mouth. A cartoon face is usually quite small, so if the artist filled it up with realistic features, the viewer might miss how the character is feeling.

In this typical manga face, you can see how the features are unrealistic. The eyes are enormous and spaced widely apart.

By focusing attention on a character's eyes and mouth, readers instantly know how the character is feeling. You can read more about how to show a character's emotions on pages 42–43.

Mass appeal

Hogan's Alley by Richard Outcault, first created in 1895, contained the first cartoon character that was widely seen and liked. The Yellow Kid, who got his name from the yellow nightshirt he wore, had a babyish, smiling, goofy face. He had simple dots or circles for eyes, small eyebrows high on his head, and big ears. His facial proportions were almost exactly the same as those of a chimp, and we know how appealing chimps are!

Although the Yellow Kid behaved badly, his innocent, playful face allowed him to get away with it.

The real deal

Many characters' faces in graphic novels meant for an older audience are drawn quite realistically. The extra length of these comics gives more space for artists to show emotions without using cartoon features. In some manga, only the main characters or heroes have simplified features.

The minor characters are given realistic faces. There is no need to stress their emotions, since they are not central to the story. Villains sometimes also have more realistic faces because the artist wants to conceal their emotions—which adds to the mystery.

Types of character

Do you recognize some of these types of cartoon character?

- Athletic, muscular heroes with special powers that help them overcome villains
- Thin, scowling villains with a habit of laughing crazily and uncontrollably
- Strong, rather stupid thugs with heavy jaws, who carry out the orders of a villain
- Mad scientists who always seem to wear glasses and lab coats, and who have unruly hair
- Bungling police officers incapable of solving crimes without the help of superheroes.

Emphasizing roles

Different comic creators draw characters in predictable ways so that readers will know just by a character's appearance what his or her role is in the story. The way a character is drawn can also help to emphasize a character's abilities. For example, the Incredible Hulk has biceps and fists at least as wide as his head because strength and power are essential to his character.

Strong characterization

In addition to drawing characters with predictable, easily recognizable features, comic artists also exaggerate the behavior of their characters. For example, heroes are often very good and want to help others, whereas villains are very bad and selfish.

Strong characterization also helps readers to identify with characters. For example, we may feel a lot of empathy with a shy, quiet teenager because we know people like that at school, or maybe that is how we feel ourselves.

Double acts

Many comic heroes, such as Batman and Robin, have **sidekicks**. These are characters the heroes may travel around with or go into battle with. Heroes and sidekicks care for each other and are always loyal. A sidekick is often more vulnerable than the hero, maybe in strength, size, or weaknesses. This allows the comic creator to invent lots of dangerous situations the sidekick needs to be saved from.

Comic teams

Sometimes one hero is not enough to save the world! Some heroes, such as the X-Men, Fantastic Four, and Power Rangers, act in teams. Each team member usually has a different special skill that complements the skills of the others. Comic creators can come up with lots of different fights against the same villain if they use a team of heroes.

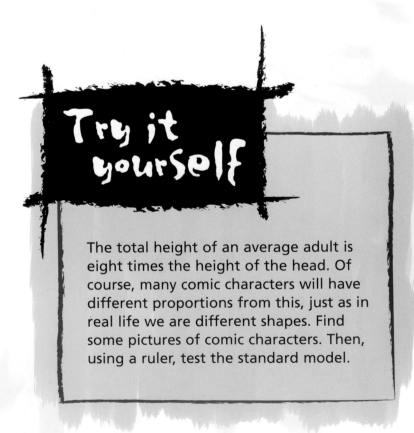

Try it yourself

The total height of an average adult is eight times the height of the head. Of course, many comic characters will have different proportions from this, just as in real life we are different shapes. Find some pictures of comic characters. Then, using a ruler, test the standard model.

The double act of Asterix and Obelix, created in 1961 by Goscinny and Uderzo, has been featured in over 30 graphic novels.

Forget-me-not

When you start to create your own comic heroes, try to come up with ways to make them stand out from the crowd. Comic artists often use unusual colors and shapes. For example, the Incredible Hulk has bright green skin. Members of the Simpson family not only have yellow skin, but also unusual hairstyles—Marge has a tower of curly blue hair and Bart has yellow spikes. Some characters' features, such as Mickey Mouse's ears, are so recognizable that even when seen alone they have become symbols of the character.

With his spiky hair and red-and-black sweater, Dennis the Menace, one of the most popular characters in the British comic *The Beano*, has a distinctive mischievous look.

A single panel

Artist Gary Larson created a unique format for his comic *The Far Side*. Each installment of *The Far Side* was a single panel with a caption and, sometimes, word bubbles. There were no regular characters. The quirky humor of these single panels made *The Far Side* very popular.

Props

You might choose to associate your main characters with particular objects, as many comic artists do. These objects are like the **props** used by characters in stage plays. Props can help define characters. Marvel and DC comics are full of these props, such as Batman's Batmobile, Wolverine's claws (in *X-Men*), Captain America's shield, and Superman's Fortress of Solitude. Such props recur throughout these series, gaining meaning and power over time.

Personal style

Most comic artists use black outlines for characters with colored-in spaces, but you can use many different media. For example, student Ben Williams uses **silhouettes** of people in different poses overlaid on background photographs. Artist Frank Masereel printed early comic strips using carved blocks of wood to give the images a jagged, homemade look.

Ben Williams's comic strip uses silhouettes of real people superimposed on photographic backgrounds to create an interesting personal style.

Try it yourself

Try experimenting with different media. Get a comic strip or graphic novel and trace a character's face. Enlarge the tracing, perhaps with a photocopier. Now, try making five large versions of the face using different media: for example, a thick marker pen, a wax crayon, paint applied with a wide brush, cut-out pieces of newspaper on white paper, and white chalk on black paper. Which do you prefer? How do the different media change the personality or feel of the character?

moving into the Panel

The characters you create exist in the space provided by panels. But they are not the only things in panels. Artists draw backgrounds to show the world the characters live in. They also have ways of showing movement through that world.

In the background

Readers concentrate on what characters are doing in a comic, so long as they are drawn well and the story is good. So, why spend a lot of time drawing a background that readers may only glance at? The point is that an accurate background, especially in the opening panel, shows the reader what the comic world looks like and where the action is taking place.

The important thing about any comic background is that it is believable. A science fiction background showing an imagined planet can be just as believable as one that accurately reproduces a real place on Earth.

When less is more

You do not have to draw a complete background in every panel. Sometimes the background is reduced to a plain color. This is to keep the reader's focus on the excitement of the action. When it is time to shift the scene, another detailed background will be necessary to show the new setting for the action.

Hergé, the creator of Tintin, studied photographs of buildings in central Kathmandu, Nepal, to create this detailed background in *Tintin in Tibet*.

Background techniques

Most comic artists know they should be just as creative with their backgrounds as they would be with their superheroes' costumes. They learn to draw backgrounds by studying and copying pictures of anything that may exist in their comic world. They learn all about **perspective**, which is the way things appear to be smaller when farther away. Using the rules of perspective makes the background look **three-dimensional** rather than flat.

Some artists spend a lot of time studying real places so they can draw them accurately. For example, Hergé researched the geography, buildings, culture, and costumes of Kathmandu, Nepal, and parts of Tibet in order to create realistic backgrounds for *Tintin in Tibet*.

Try it yourself

Comic **composition** is the art of arranging background, characters, and word bubbles within a panel so they make sense. Each panel should have one center of interest, be it a character or event. This does not need to be in the middle of the panel. Other things in the panel should be positioned to help focus attention on the center of interest. Try to compose three panels each featuring a church, a hero, and a villain, but with different centers of interest.

Slowing the pace

How do artists control the pace of the action in a comic? One way to do this is by varying the width of the panels. Using a wider panel than normal can slow the pace down. A wide panel forces closure between panels to happen more slowly. This is because it takes longer to look at a wide panel before you can move on to the next.

Including a lot of detail in a panel also slows down the pace of the action, since it takes the reader more time to take the panel in. Another way to slow down the pace is to repeat almost identical panels. This shows the reader nothing has changed and therefore the action has slowed.

Speeding up

Conversely, an artist can speed up the pace by placing many narrow panels together or even by showing a clock or calendar in one panel and then showing it changed by a certain time period in the next panel.

Moving pictures

Things within comic panels cannot move, but we can draw them in a way that makes them look as if they are moving. Comic artists can draw **motion lines** to suggest movement. These are streaks from the edge of a moving subject back in the direction the subject moved from. The background is drawn in focus. The lines are arcs in the case of, say, a swinging fist, or straight lines for, say, a rocket taking off or a car speeding past.

Manga artists were the first to draw moving subjects against blurred or very streaky backgrounds. This technique is now widespread in modern comics because it makes readers feel they are moving, too. Readers are therefore likely to get more involved in the story.

Motion lines were more common than blurs in traditionally drawn comics because they are easier to produce in ink on paper. However, blurs can be created easily today at the click of a few buttons using computer drawing software.

Try it yourself

Try making your comic characters appear to move. Using a soft pencil, draw a wide panel and a running character near its right-hand edge. It should look as if it is running from left to right.

Fill in some sort of background, such as a row of trees or houses. Hold an eraser against the paper just behind the left-hand edge of the character's outline. Now, flick and lift the eraser in a smooth stroke toward the left. Repeat this until the background is slightly blurred.

In this manga panel, it is the background that has motion lines rather than the motorcycles and riders. We see the background as a blur, as the moving characters would.

Points of view

Have you ever sat through a relative's lengthy wedding or vacation video—one of those videos where all the action is filmed from exactly the same position? It can get pretty boring. The reason for this is that in real life we constantly change how closely we look at things. We also change our position and the angle from which we view things.

Comic artists use different views in panels to make the world within more believable and more interesting to look at. For example, if you were to show two people sitting at a table talking, rather than always using a side view, you could make it more interesting by using a different view in each panel. You could also try showing what each person sees, such as the other person's face and open mouth.

Look at the way manga artist Osamu Tezuka has mixed up the points of view in the comic strip to add interest for the viewer.

Hot shots

"**Shot**" is the general term for a type of view. The term comes from filmmaking, where action is said to be "shot." Here are some major shot types:

● **Close-up shots:** These are used to show details, emotions, reactions, and expressions—for example, beads of sweat running down a nervous character's forehead.

● **Medium shots:** These are used to help viewers get to know what the characters look like and to show body language—for example, one character sneaking up on another character from behind.

● **Long shots:** These are used to show settings, location of things in those settings, and large-scale action involving many characters—for example, soldiers in a fort seeing clouds of dust from approaching, distant warriors.

● **Low-angle shots:** These show a view from lower than eye level and are used to distort or add strength and size to subjects—for example, looking up from ground level at a tall monster or building.

● **High-angle shots:** These show a view from higher than eye level and are used to reduce the strength or size of a subject or to show a character observing action—for example, a boy hiding safely up a tree, while watching villains searching for him.

Try it yourself

You may need to draw lots of guidelines to get the vertical positions of facial features correct from different angles.

If you want to use different shots, you will probably need to know what your characters look like from all angles. A good way to learn is to draw a "turn-around." Draw a strip of five panels, and in the first draw a head from the front. Then, draw horizontal guidelines across the strip marking the levels at which facial features begin and end—for example, the top of an ear or the start of the hair. Then, using your guidelines, draw the head partly turned to you, from the side, partly turned away, and from the back.

making Comics effective

Most of us know what a difference sound makes to life, from music and speech to the sounds of things happening all around us. A comic or graphic novel does not make any noise, but creators have ways of adding **sound effects** using words and symbols. They also use color and light effects to change the moods in their created worlds.

The art of noise

At the beginning of the 20th century, movies were silent. The words actors spoke were written down in caption slides shown in gaps between the action. Live music, which was often played on pianos as movies were shown, added atmosphere to on-screen action.

Comics are a bit like silent movies. In the earliest comics, words were usually written underneath panels. Today, however, any speech and sound effects that accompany the action are usually included within the panel.

Composing with bubbles

Word bubbles contain the words that comic characters speak or think. Word bubbles generally have arrows to point to the speaker, but **thought bubbles** may have a row of smaller circles leading to the thinker. Knowing who says or thinks what is essential, especially if there are several speakers in one panel. The bubbles are sometimes overlapping and interconnected to help the reader know the order in which to read them. The space occupied by bubbles in a panel varies with the amount spoken and the number of characters speaking. Artists need to make sure that the bubbles do not obscure the action.

In early examples of the Yellow Kid (see page 27), words appeared on the baby's shirt. Eventually the Yellow Kid's creator, Richard Outcault, started to use word bubbles, and this trend continued in most other popular comics of the early 20th century and beyond.

Try it yourself

On page 39 is a comic strip showing some dialogue between two characters, Beaver and Steve, drawn by James Turner. Get a sheet of tracing paper and copy the panels, leaving the bubbles blank. Now, try changing the dialogue. This time maybe Beaver could talk about the price of bananas or why he doesn't like zoos!

Now, trace the panels with your dialogue in the word bubbles, but without the characters Beaver and Steve. Draw in your own characters to fit the conversation.

The layout of word bubbles in these *Beaver and Steve* panels helps you follow the order of the dialogue.

For emphasis

If you have ever listened to good storytellers, you know that they do not speak at the same volume or speed all the time. They emphasize some words to help tell their story. Comic artists can stress the importance of words by making them look different from others in a panel. For example, they can be in *italics*, CAPITALS, or **bold** letters.

Sound effects

There are always lots of noises all around us, such as the drone of cars on a road or the sound of coughing and scraping chairs in class. We only notice some of these noises when they are not there. Other sounds, such as bangs or crashes, immediately grab our attention. The action in a comic would be very lifeless without sound effects such as these.

A brief history of writing

Writing with letters is fairly recent in human history. The first writing was done by Sumerian people over 8,000 years ago, but they used pictograms, which are simple pictures that look like familiar objects such as mountains. Later on, the ancient Egyptians used symbols called hieroglyphics to represent ideas, such as an ox to indicate food (meat). It was not until 3,000 years ago that civilizations developed alphabets of letters, which are symbols that mean sounds.

Each of these hieroglyphic symbols has a meaning. For example, in the first column the wavy lines mean water or liquid and the bird next to the plant means "to adore."

Imitating sounds

Some sound effects are easy to convert into words, such as the "ding-dong" of a doorbell. Others are more difficult. For example, how would you write down the noise made by a pin landing on a hard floor or by someone doing a belly flop? Comic creators are often inventive in making words that imitate the sounds of the action they represent.

Onomatopoeia

Imitating sounds in this way is called **onomatopoeia**. For example, sound effects such as "Pow!" and "Sock!" are often used in fight scenes. Sounds are often given extra emphasis by how they are drawn. For example, the word "screek," used to indicate the sound of claws scraping across metal, might be drawn in jagged letters.

Comic artists often use outsize words to create the impression of very loud sounds, as in this panel from *The Fantastic Mr. Grant* web comic by artist Steve Galgas.

Try it yourself

See if you can make up some words for these sounds that you could put into your comic panels: paper ripping, thunder, a cat scratching the carpet, stirring hot chocolate, and a modem dialing.

Thought and mood symbols

Comic artists often use symbols instead of words in bubbles to express thoughts and moods. These are called **emanata**. They use emanata because it is quicker and takes less space than words. They rely on readers having seen the symbols before and recognizing their meanings. Here are just a few:

- ? = "what on earth is going on?"
- $$ = "this is going to make me rich"
- 💡 = "I've had an idea"
- circle of flying birds = "I'm feeling knocked out"
- halo of sweat droplets = "I'm feeling anxious."

The trouble with symbols is that they sometimes only mean something to particular audiences. For example, in Japan dreaming is generally shown as a bubble emerging from the nose of a comic character. This might be completely lost on a non-Japanese reader, who may think the character simply has a cold!

Let's face it

One look at a friend's face and we can usually tell if the friend is sad or happy. Slight differences in the shapes of eyebrows and lips, pupil size, and forehead lines tell us a lot about people's moods. It can be tricky to show complicated moods on the small face of a comic character. However, if you draw your faces manga-style, with enormous eyes, then the possibilities of showing mood are greater.

Try it yourself

Try drawing and practicing manga moods! Buy or borrow a manga comic book or graphic novel and look at the shapes of the characters' eyes and mouths. You should be able to see that different emotions such as sadness and happiness are usually drawn in particular ways. Use the following tips:

- *Sadness:* The eyebrows are angled upward away from the ears, with the inner tips almost vertical. The eyes are rounded, with the upper and lower eyelids curving upward. The small mouth curves downward.

- *Happiness:* The eyelids are as in a sad expression. The eyebrows are farther away from the eyes and their inner tips do not curve up at a different angle. The eyes have large pupils and **glints**, which are white blobs showing reflected light. The open mouth is smiling.

- *Anger:* The eyebrows are low down, close to the eyes, and angle upward away from the nose. The mouth curves downward.

- *Shock:* The eyes are open wide with tiny pupils and the mouth is very small and O-shaped.

Sadness

Happiness

Anger

Shock

GRHAWAARRH!

Help! Fire! Murder! Whatever shall I do?

HAWAARRH!

Action stations! Full steam ahead! Charge!

HWAAARRH!

Hang on, Tintin!... Here I come!...

The emanata used in this page from *Tintin in Tibet* help show a range of feelings in the characters, from anxiety and fear to confusion and surprise.

43

Out of the shadows

On Halloween, most of us have probably shone a flashlight up from below our faces to scare our friends. **Uplighting** makes faces look strange because the light comes from the opposite direction from normal downward **light sources**, such as sunlight. Uplighting is just one of the lighting effects comic artists can use to add mystery to their stories.

Backlighting, showing light coming from behind, defines the silhouette of a character or object but not its surface detail, so the character's identity may be unclear. For example, a door crashes open and a backlit character stands there. Is it a hero or a villain? Reducing the amount of light on a character's face makes facial expressions and moods difficult to spot. Large areas of black in backgrounds can be used to suggest danger lurking in the shadows.

Try it yourself

Try practicing lighting effects to create different moods. Draw a cartoon character with details such as facial features and clothing. Repeat the figure several times by tracing, photocopying, or scanning. Then, add a light effect to each, such as a strong light from above or below or weak candlelight from behind. Think carefully about what would be in shadow and what would be lit up. Look at photos and paintings in magazines, newspapers, or comics to help you. What different moods have you created?

Color moods

Comic artists use color in panels to create moods. For example, using lots of blue can make a scene appear calm, cool, or truthful, whereas lots of red brings energy, excitement, and sometimes aggression. Moebius is the comic name for the French artist Jean Giraud. He uses a lot of light shades of purple and lilac in his graphic novels to give a surreal quality to the stories.

Sources and surfaces

Street lights or the Sun are not the only light sources. Light comes from lots of other places, such as cell phones, computer screens, candles, explosions, and dashboards. These lights have different colors and strengths. Artists need to be creative to make light sources in their panels appear realistic. This is made more challenging because light reflects differently depending on what surfaces it shines on.

Shiny surfaces such as metal, glass, water, and eyes reflect light very well. They need to be drawn with glints in the right places. Dull or matt surfaces such as tarmac or skin reflect light very little when dry but more so when wet.

In this *Beaver and Steve* comic strip, notice the way that artist James Turner has used lighting as well as bright colors and black to help create a dramatic effect.

Getting into Comics

Do you find yourself doodling comic strips? Are you committed to drawing perfect manga faces? Does the journey from first idea to finished panels excite you? Well, it sounds as if you are up for the challenge of becoming a comic creator.

Practice, practice, practice

If you play an instrument, you need to learn your scales. If you are on a basketball team, you need to practice shooting baskets. Creating comics is just the same. You might be good at drawing already, but putting together comics that will interest readers takes practice. So, get yourself a sketchbook or two and develop your skills. Here are some ideas:

● Draw objects such as balls, fruits, and skateboards from lots of different viewpoints and lit by different light sources. Your aim is to see how different shapes change when viewed in different ways. Draw in soft pencil to show shading and make the objects appear three-dimensional.

● Visit a natural history museum. Draw the skeletons of animals to understand how their shapes are different. How many variations on the same theme of spine, skull, and limbs can you spot?

● Copy panels featuring your favorite comic characters. Use black ink for outlines and add color. Concentrate on the body shapes, facial expressions, background perspective, and lighting. Then, try drawing your own panels featuring these characters.

Learn from others, be yourself

Borrow, buy, or browse as many comics and graphic novels as you can to see how others do it. But aim to be yourself and create a comic world of your own. Start by developing your own characters. Make notes about what they are like and how they would react in different situations. Think of the world they live in and the other characters and dangers they might face in that world. Then, jot down some story ideas, convert these into scripts, and do some rough layouts. Finally, draw your characters in panels, adding other elements such as word bubbles and motion lines.

One of the best ways of seeing a wide range of comics and graphic novels is by going to a comic fair.

Keep a reference

To be a comic artist you may need to draw just about anything. So, start a picture reference file. Cut out images from old magazines and newspapers. Take a camera with you when you go out and photograph anything from fire engines to phone booths. Use the Internet, too. Need to draw a marmoset's eyes or a Samurai's sword? Search online ...

Creating a comic portfolio

The aim of all your practice should be to create a comic portfolio. You can include your best copies of Batman panels, but the portfolio is mostly a showcase for a wide range of comic-creating skills. You want to show others that:

● You can tell a story well using a sequence of panels

● You can draw convincing comic worlds for your characters to inhabit

● You can show emotions and drama in the faces of your characters.

Generally, you should include your best and most recent work.

It is a good idea to get into the habit of showing others your work. Show art teachers, friends, and family. See which of your creations get the best reactions from your audience. Why not also include the exercises you have completed from the "Try it yourself" features in this book?

Get out more

Comic creators learn about drawing and stories from many sources. When you visit a gallery or art museum, don't just think about which pictures you like. Look at the composition and the colors used. When you go to see a movie, don't just follow the story. Look at how scenes are used to break up the action, the positioning of people on screen, and how camera angles and lighting affect mood.

The editor of Marvel's *X-Men* reviews the portfolio of an aspiring comic artist at a comic fair in Philadelphia.

Going further

You have your portfolio, so what next? Many budding comic creators plan to go off to college to study illustration or art when they leave high school. The portfolio is very useful to show the college what you can do.

Courses of study vary greatly, but will probably involve learning how to use different media to create comics, how to use computer drawing software, scripting, and layout, and how to create comics that sell. You will certainly meet and share ideas with other enthusiastic comic creators, both students and professionals.

Creator focus: Erin Flanagan

Erin Flanagan is a college student studying illustration. In 2005 students from her college got together with a professional comic artist to make their own comic book, called *Ace Comics*. Erin says:

"The professional advice on our work was very useful. It got me thinking in terms of the overall project from start to finish—developing an idea and taking it to completion. It's strange seeing my work in such a professional-looking publication, but really good, too, because it's all about getting your ideas out there."

Comic careers

First, the bad news: of all the people who complete illustration and art classes in college, very few get jobs as comic creators. Now, the good news: the ability to simplify stories into pictures and small amounts of text is in demand. Many people with comic backgrounds go into jobs in advertising and marketing, become children's book illustrators, get into TV or movie production, or teach art themselves.

Some comic creators get jobs in comic publishing houses. Many of these start out with fairly simple jobs such as adding color to other people's outlines. However, if your ideas are strong enough, you may be lucky enough to get a commission to write or draw your own comics for publication. That is one reason it is important to continually update your portfolio. If a chance of more interesting work comes up, you can show what you can do right away.

Going it alone

It is very expensive to produce final artwork, print, and distribute finished comic books.

So, most publishers get together a few sample pages of panels to show at book fairs to build up interest in their books before completing the rest. They may change comics to help them sell—for example, by editing rambling stories into shorter, snappier ones or by changing the appearance of characters they think will not be popular. Some comic creators decide to publish their own work to keep creative control over what they produce. The downside is that they do not get paid until they have something to sell, and a large comic may take months or even years to complete.

Spin-offs

Just imagine if one of your comic creations became as popular as Spiderman. The most successful comic creations are in great demand to help sell products ranging from breakfast cereals to towels. Some even get transformed into animated or live-action movies shown around the world. The rewards for comic creators are great. You could even end up drawing further adventures of your characters for years to come!

Different roles

When you create a comic at home, you will usually do everything, from finding a story to layout and final artwork. In comic publishing houses, however, different artists often have different roles in a team. For example, "pencillers" create rough shapes of characters in layouts and "inkers" turn sketches into finished artwork.

Comics have inspired many people who have careers working on animated feature films. Mr. Incredible and his superhero family in *The Incredibles* have powers and costumes similar to some familiar comic book superheroes.

Glossary

allegory work in which the story, characters, or events have symbolic meanings assigned to them

autobiographical entirely or partly dealing with the writer's own life

background part of a scene (or picture) that lies behind objects in the foreground

backlighting showing a light source from behind something

backstory action and events that took place before the present events of the story

brainstorming problem-solving technique that involves creating a list that includes a wide variety of related ideas

caption heading, title, or other explanation about an illustration

caricature drawing that exaggerates prominent features or characteristics of a subject

close-up shot detailed view of a subject that fills a panel or movie frame

closure way we observe the parts but imagine the whole—for example, by filling in the gaps in the action between one image and the next in a comic

comic book magazine or book containing the sequential art form of comics. Comic books are sometimes called comics or comic albums.

comic strip short strip or sequence of drawings that tell a story

composition plan, placement, or arrangement of the elements of art in a work

computer graphics software program that pictorially represents and manipulates data

dialogue words that characters say to each other

emanata symbols used instead of words to express thoughts and moods

epilepsy disorder of the nervous system that can result in episodes of severe convulsions with loss of consciousness

glints white shapes in shiny surfaces to show reflected light

graphics tablet device that allows you to draw images directly into a computer. It consists of a small board on which you write or draw using a pen-like stylus. As you draw, the image is displayed on the computer screen.

gutter gap between two comic panels

high-angle shot view of a subject or action from above eye level

high-resolution sharp and highly detailed

layout arrangement of panels on a page of a comic book

light source position from which the light comes

long shot view of a subject from a distance, showing its location

low-angle shot view of a subject or action from below eye level

manga Japanese comics characterized by a typical style of drawing and subject matter

manipulate change the form or position of an object

medium specific type of artistic technique

medium shot view of part of a subject, such as a person from the waist up

motion lines drawn lines that suggest movement in an illustration

onomatopoeia when words sound like the noises they represent

panel space bounded by lines containing characters, background, and other elements in a comic

perspective technique used by artists to show the relationship between close and distant objects

portfolio collection of pieces of creative work to show to potential employers or educators

prop movable article or objects used by characters in a comic, play, or movie

Pulitzer Prize annual award for achievements in U.S. journalism, letters, drama, and music

scene set of actions or dialogue that takes place in one location and at one time in a story

script detailed written description of a story that includes scene-by-scene dialogue, action, and instructions on how to represent it

sequential art two or more pictures positioned side-by-side in a deliberate sequence in order to tell a story

Shonen type of manga with characters and action suitable for young teenage boys

shot type of view—for example, a close-up

sidekick close companion who assists a main character

silhouette dark image outlined against a lighter background

sound effects words imitating sounds needed in a comic, such as "boom" for an explosion

superhero type of character who is good and has special abilities

surreal strange or bizarre

syndicated sold to appear in different places. Comic strips, news stories, and photos may be syndicated in different newspapers.

synopsis short summary of a story or script

template pre-designed format for text and graphics on which new text or pages can be based

thought bubble rounded shape containing words that represent thoughts of characters in a comic

three-dimensional having height, width, and depth

uplighting when a light source is below a character or object

word bubble rounded shape containing words spoken by characters in a comic

Find Out More

Comics and graphic novels

Here are just a few sources of inspiration you will find:

Action Comics (featuring Superman). New York: DC Comics, first issued in 1938.

Eisner, Will. *Life on Another Planet*. Amherst, Mass.: Kitchen Sink, 1996.

Gaiman, Neil. *Books of Magic* (series). New York: DC Comics, 1993.

Goscinny, René, and Albert Uderzo. *Asterix* (series). New York: Dargaud, first published 1960s.

Hergé. *The Adventures of Tintin* (over 20 separate titles). Boston: Little, Brown, 1990s.

Lee, Stan. *The Ultimate Spider-Man*. New York: Berkley, 1994.

Marz, Ron. *Marvel vs. DC*. New York: DC Comics, 1996. Hulk vs. Superman!

Medley, Linda. *Castle Waiting*. Seattle: Fantagraphics, 2006. A group of eccentric characters who live in a castle.

Miller, Frank. *Batman: Dark Knight Returns* or *Batman: Year One*. New York: Warner, 1986 or 1988.

Miyazaki, Hayao. *Nausicaa of the Valley of Wind* (7-volume series). San Francisco: Viz, 2004. A good example of manga.

Pilkey, Dav. *Captain Underpants and the Perilous Plot of Professor Poopypants*. New York: Scholastic, 2000.

Rucka, Greg, and Ed Brubaker, art by Michael Lark. *Gotham Central*. New York: DC Comics, 2004.

Satrapi, Marjane. *Persepolis: The Story of an Iranian Childhood*. New York: Pantheon, 2003.

Shanower, Eric. *Age of Bronze* (series). Orange, Calif.: Image Comics, first published 2000. Graphic novel versions of the Trojan War based on famous accounts of the war, originally told by the ancient Greek poet Homer.

Simone, Gail, art by Dale Eaglesham and Wade von Grawbadger. *Villains United* (6-volume series). New York: DC Comics, 2005.

Smith, Jeff. *Bone* (series). Columbus, Ohio: Cartoon Books, 1996. A cross between Tolkein and the Smurfs!

Spiegelman, Art. *Maus I* & *Maus II*. New York: Penguin/Random House & Pantheon, 1986.

Superman. New York: DC Comics, first issued in 1939.

Tezuka, Osamu. *Astro Boy* (graphic novel series). New York: Watson-Guptill, from 2002.

Toriyama, Akira. *Dragonball Z* (graphic novel series). San Francisco: Viz, from 2000.

Veitch, Tom. *Star Wars: Dark Empire*. Milwaukie, Ore.: Dark Horse Comics, 1993.

Resource books

Amara, Philip, and Pop Mhan. *So You Wanna Be a Comic Book Artist?* Hillsboro, Ore.: Beyond Words, 2001.

Coope, Katy. *How to Draw Manga: A Step-by-Step Guide.* New York: Tangerine, 2002. Written by a 17-year-old fan of manga.

Eisner, Will. *Comics and Sequential Art.* Tamarac, Fla.: Poorhouse, 2000.

Giarrano, Vincent. *Comics Crash Course.* Cincinatti: Impact, 2004.

Hart, Christopher. *Christopher Hart's Portable Cartoon Studio/Kit: Instruction Book.* New York: Watson-Guptill, 1996.

Hogarth, Burne. *Dynamic Figure Drawing.* New York: Watson-Guptill, 1996.

Janson, Klaus. *The DC Comics Guide to Inking Comics.* New York: Watson-Guptill, 2003.

Janson, Klaus. *The DC Comics Guide to Pencilling Comics.* New York: Watson-Guptill, 2002.

McCloud, Scott. *Understanding Comics: The Invisible Art.* New York: HarperCollins, 1994.

Watson, B. S. *Dragonball Z* (*How to Draw* series). New York: Scholastic, 2002.

Useful websites

http://www.artstudiollc.com
The official website of the author and artist Christopher Hart, who has written many instruction books for comic artists.

http://dccomics.com
The official website of DC Comics, publishers of many comics and graphic novels, including comics featuring Superman and Batman.

http://en-f.tezuka.co.jp/
Online information about the works of the Japanese manga artist Osamu Tezuka.

http://marvel.com
The website of Marvel Comics, publishers of many comics and graphic novels, including comics featuring Spiderman and the Incredible Hulk.

http://www.mycomicbookcreator.com
A website with a free trial of *Comic Book Creator* (*PlanetWide Games, 2005*), an easy-to-use software package that you can use to create your own comic books on a computer.

http://www.pilkey.com/index.php
The website of the creator of the comic *Captain Underpants*, Dav Pilkey. Includes information about Dav Pilkey's books plus fun games to play.

http://www.scholastic.com/captainunderpants
The online adventures of Captain Underpants. You can even make your own Captain Underpants comics!

http://www.willeisner.com/indexnormal.html
The official website of artist Will Eisner, creator of the comic *The Spirit*.

Disclaimer
All the Internet addresses (URLs) given in this book were valid at the time of going to press. However, owing to the dynamic nature of the Internet, some addresses may have changed or sites may have ceased to exist since publication. While the author, packager, and publishers regret any inconvenience this may cause readers, no responsibility for any such change can be accepted by the author, packager, or publisher.

Index